D1534640

Fun Things
to Do with
Paper Cups
and Plates

by Kara L. Laughlin

A+ Books are published by Capstone Press,
1710 Roe Crest Drive, North Mankato, Minnesota 56003
www.capstonepub.com

Library of Congress Cataloging-in-Publication Data
Laughlin, Kara L.
Fun Things to Do with Paper Cups and Plates/by Kara L. Laughlin.
pages cm.—(A+ Books. 10 Things to Do)
Includes bibliographical references.
Summary: "Full-color photos and simple, step-by-step instructions describe 10 crafts and activities using paper cups, paper plates, and common materials found around the house"—Provided by publisher.
Audience: Age 5–8.
Audience: K to grade 3.
ISBN 978-1-4765-9897-0 (library binding)
ISBN 978-1-4765-9901-4 (ebook pdf)
1. Paper work—Juvenile literature. 2. Handicraft—Juvenile literature. 3. Paper plates—Juvenile literature. I. Title.
TT870.L3268 2015
745.5—dc23   2014012745

Editorial Credits
Jeni Wittrock, editor; Bobbie Nuytten, designer; Sarah Schuette, photo stylist; Marcy Morin, studio scheduler; Kim Braun, project production; Tori Abraham, production specialist

Photo Credits
Images by Capstone Studio: Karon Dubke except Shutterstock: Eskemar, 16 (right), Hal_P, 28, Melica, 6 (t), Silberkorn, 10 (t), whitemaple, 20 (t), Wiktoria Pawlak, 12 (b), wind moon, 26

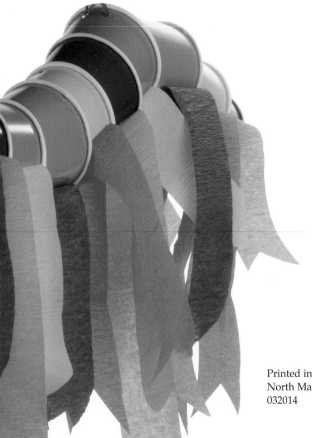

Printed in the United States of America in
North Mankato, Minnesota
032014   008087CGF14

Table of Contents

Introduction

Chances are, there are paper plates and cups in your kitchen. If you're only using them for picnics and pizza, you're missing out! Did you know you can make art with them and music too? You can even turn them into toys.

You might have everything you need for these projects at home. If not, you can find what you need at a craft store. And party stores have a rainbow of choices for colored paper plates and cups.

Have fun with the projects in this book. When you've made them all, think up some cool projects of your own!

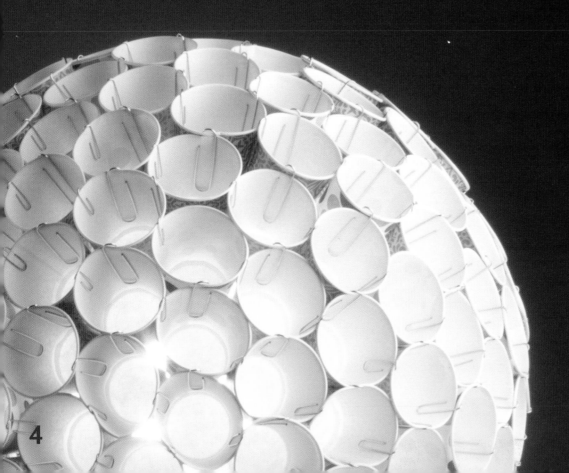

Catch a Button

Supplies

» paper cup
» pencil
» 18 inches (0.5 meter) of string or yarn
» big button
» small button

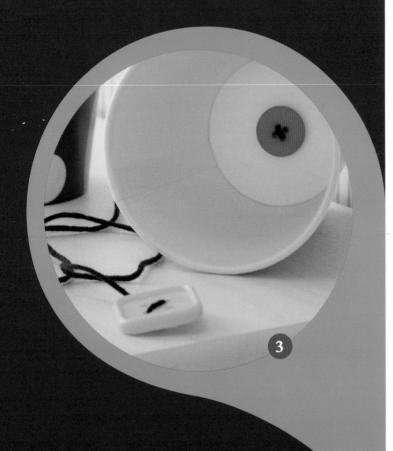

3

1 With a pencil, make a hole in the bottom of a cup.

2 Thread the string through the hole.

3 Tie a button to each end of the string. The small button should sit inside the cup. The big button hangs down.

4 Now give it a try! Swing the big button out and catch it in the cup. It's a little tricky at first—don't give up!

Step it Up: When you can catch the button most of the time, try using a longer string. Is it harder or easier to win? What about a shorter string? A smaller button?

Pop-Up Portrait

Supplies

» crayons or markers
» paper plates
» hole punch
» scissors
» colored paper
» glue

1 In the middle of a paper plate, draw an animal or a person.

2 Make an opening for your scissors by punching a hole in the plate.

3 Cut out the top half of the background. Leave the plate's rim in place.

4 Fold the plate rim back. Your drawing will stand up like a picture frame.

5 Decorate the plate by gluing on paper cutouts.

Step it Up: Make a portrait of everyone in your family. Don't forget the pets!

Run a Marble

Supplies

» 3–10 paper plates
» scissors
» tape
» building blocks and other items for support
» marbles

1 Cut the rims away from two or three plates.

2 Tape the rims to blocks to make a curved track.

3 Test your track by pushing a marble from the top.

4 To help the marble stay on the track, fold the plate rim in a V. You can also tape two rims together.

5 If the marble falls off the track, don't worry. Just keep trying.

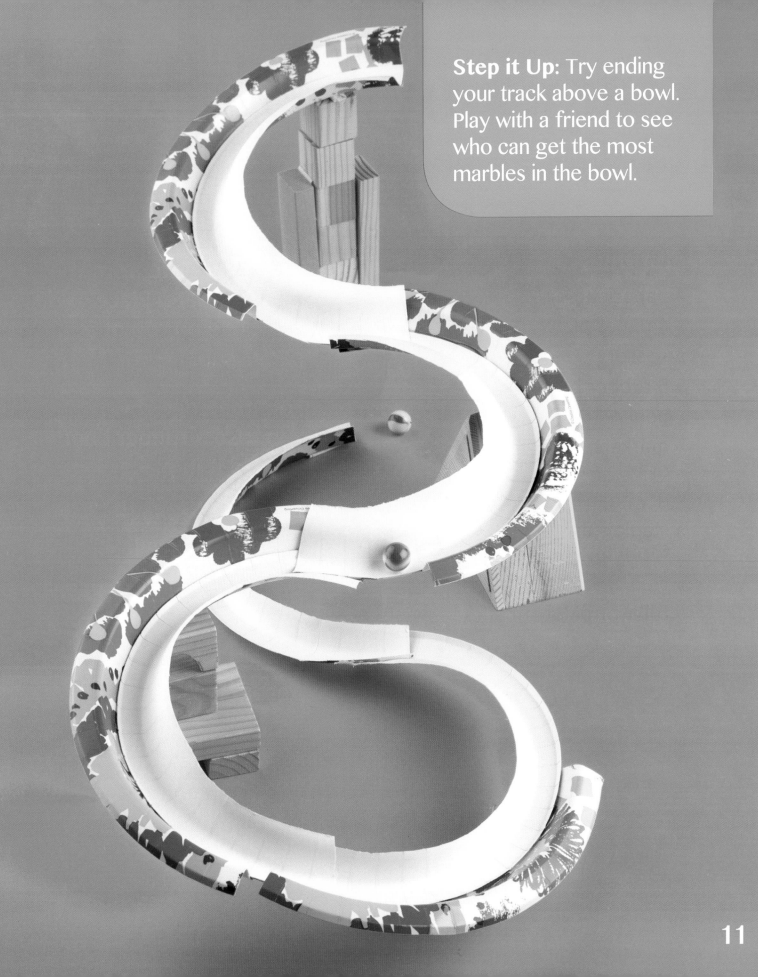

11

Step it Up: Try ending your track above a bowl. Play with a friend to see who can get the most marbles in the bowl.

Make Some Noise

Supplies

» paper cup
» 4 paper plates
» scissors
» 5 rubber bands
» pencil
» markers, stickers, or other decorations
» dry beans
» stapler (ask an adult for help)
» glue
» ruler or paint stir stick

Drum

1. Cut a big circle from a paper plate. Place the circle on top of a paper cup.

2. Fold the edges over the cup. Use a rubber band to hold it in place.

3. Tap the plate with your hand or a pencil.

Shaker

1. Decorate the bottom of a paper plate.

2. Place a handful of dry beans in the plate.

3. Staple the plate into a half circle. (Ask an adult for help.)

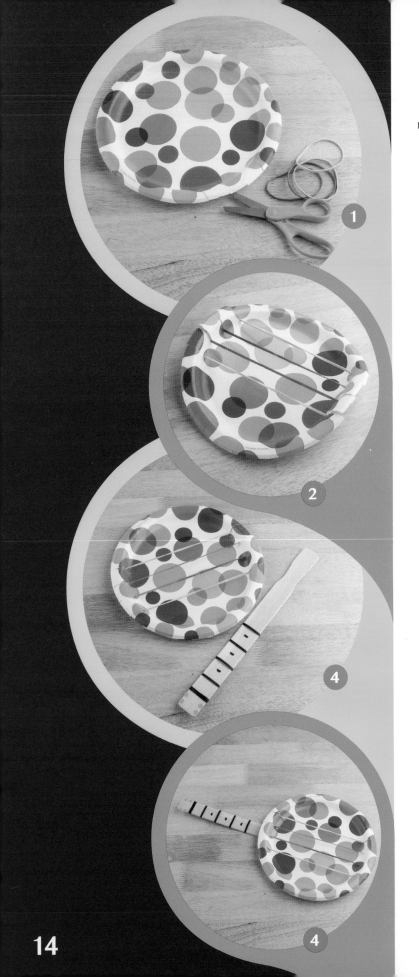

Two-Sided Banjo

1 Cut four pairs of small slits on opposite sides of a paper plate.

2 Cut each rubber band apart. Stretch one rubber band through each pair of slits.

3 Staple both ends of each rubber band to the back of the plate.

4 Glue a second plate beneath the first plate. They will fit together perfectly. While the glue dries, decorate the stir stick or ruler.

5 Glue the stick to your banjo. Let dry and strum away!

Step it Up:
Put on a parade! March through the house or down the street. Bring extra instruments so friends can join in as you go.

Box Up Lunch

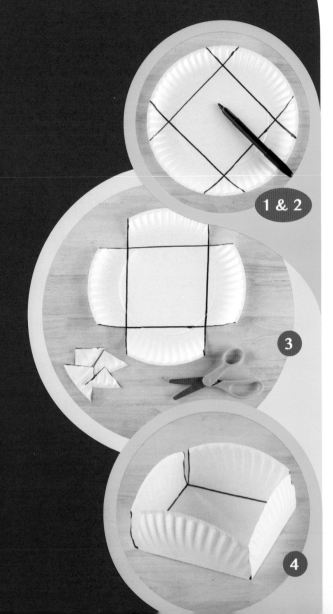

1 & 2

3

4

1. Across the center of a plate, draw two lines as shown.

2. Turn your plate 1/4 turn. Draw two more lines like the first pair. Your lines will look like a tic-tac-toe board with a big center square.

3. Cut out the four triangles in the corners.

4. Fold up the sides of the plate on the lines of the center square.

5. Tape or tie ribbon around the box to hold it together.

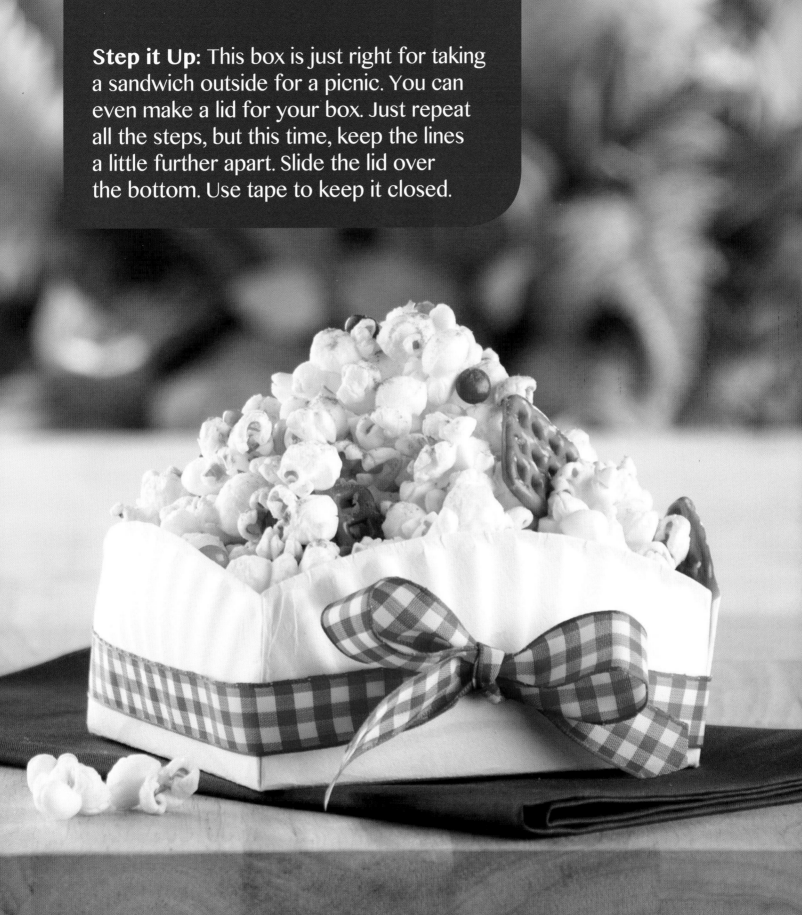

Step it Up: This box is just right for taking a sandwich outside for a picnic. You can even make a lid for your box. Just repeat all the steps, but this time, keep the lines a little further apart. Slide the lid over the bottom. Use tape to keep it closed.

Get Fishy

Supplies

» paper plates
» scissors
» glue
» stick-on wiggle eyes
» markers

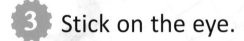

1 Cut a wedge from a paper plate to make your fish's mouth.

2 Glue the point of the wedge to the back of the fish for a tail.

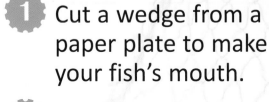

3 Stick on the eye.

4 Draw fins and scales on the plate to create your fish.

Step it Up: Tape string to your fish and get a big box to make an aquarium. Set the box on its side, and hang the fish from the top. Draw an underwater scene on paper and tape it to the back of the box.

Let's Grow!

Supplies

» paper cup
» handful of gravel
» damp soil
» moss or other small plants
» 2 or 3 small rocks or toys
» clear plastic cup

1 Put a little gravel in the paper cup for drainage.

2 Fill the cup with damp soil.

3 Set damp moss on the soil, green side up. If you can't find moss, a small plant will work too.

4 Place rocks or small toys on the soil.

5 Cover your garden with the clear cup.

6 Keep your garden in a sunny room.

Your garden won't need much watering. The cover helps keep it moist. After a month lift the cover and check the soil. If it feels dry, add a spoonful of water and check again in a few days.

Step it Up: Make a larger garden in a fish bowl or other large, clear container. Add a few different plants and mosses, toys, and figures to make a fun scene. Or, try making a desert scene with plants that like dry conditions, like cactus and aloe vera plants.

21

Build Some Curves

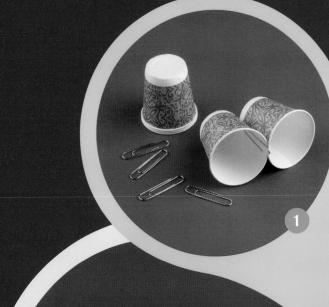

1 Slide a paper clip over the rims of two cups.

2 Use another clip to add a third cup.

3 Keep adding cups. Clip the rims together wherever they touch.

4 Make a sphere of cups but leave one small portion unfinished.

5 Place the sphere over a battery-powered lamp and watch it glow from within!

Step it Up: Make a complete sphere of cups and take it outside with a friend. Can you roll the sphere? Try playing a very gentle game of catch!

Make a Dragon

Supplies

» 11 paper cups
» pencil
» paper tubes cut into 10 2-inch (5-centimeter) rings
» string
» tape
» hole punch
» ribbon or paper streamers
» markers, paper, or stickers for dragon's face

1. Use a pencil to poke a hole in the bottom of each cup.

2. Thread the string in a cup-tube-cup-tube pattern, ending with a cup.

3. Tape the string to the first and last cups.

4. Punch holes in the top edge of the first and eighth cups.

5. Tie strings through these holes, then tie the strings to the pencil.

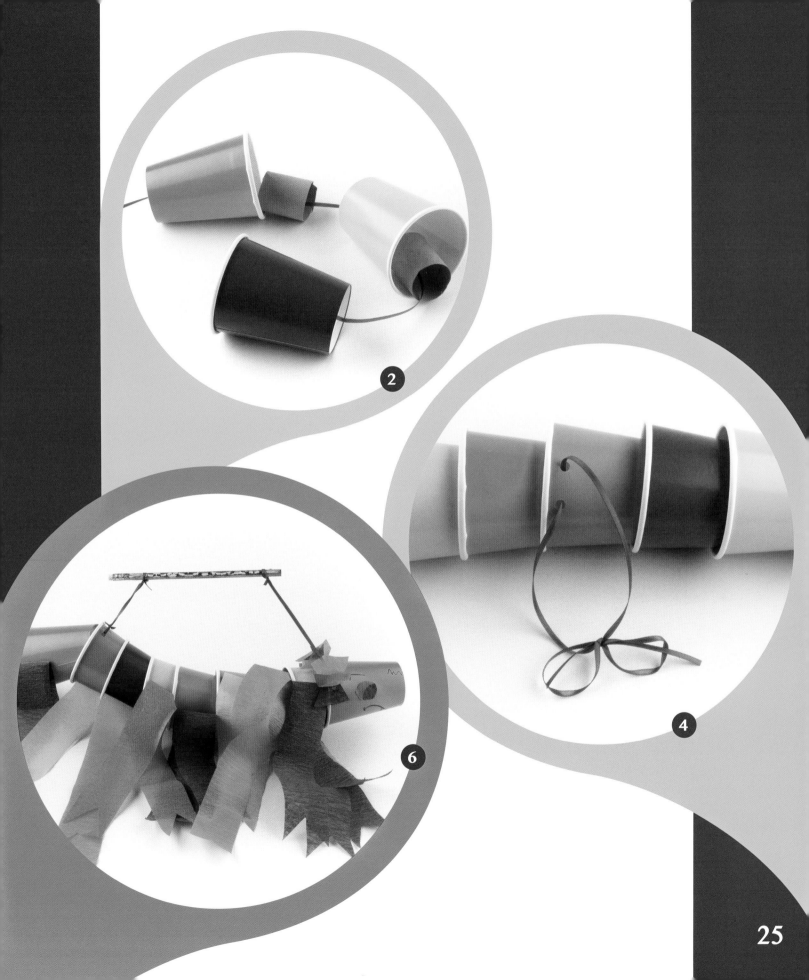

Did you know?

This dragon looks a little bit like the ones that are used to celebrate the Chinese New Year. Those dragons are puppets too. They are so big that many people must work together to make them dance.

6 Use stickers or markers to make the dragon's face.

7 Tape streamers to the dragon's mouth and sides.

8 Hold your dragon by the pencil to make it dance.

Give a Gift

Supplies

» paper cup
» scissors
» small gift
» stickers or pens
» plain sticker
» stickers, bows, or ribbon

1 Cut off the rim of your cup.

2 Cut slits around the cup to make tabs. They should end about 1/3 of the way down the cup.

3 Put your gift in the cup.

4 Go around the circle, folding each tab down. Tuck the corner of the last tab under the first.

5 If desired, use a plain sticker to make a gift tag. Place it over the folded tabs on top of the cup.

6 Decorate the gift cup with stickers, bows, or ribbon.

Step it Up: Plan a paper cup gift exchange. Each guest brings a decorated gift cup with a small gift inside. Everyone chooses a gift to open!

31

Read More

Laughlin, Kara L. *Fun Things to Do with Egg Cartons.* A+ Books. North Mankato, Minn.: Capstone Press, 2015.

Llimós, Anna. *Earth-Friendly Crafts from Recycled Stuff in 5 Easy Steps.* Earth-Friendly Crafts in Five Easy Steps. Berkeley Heights, N.J.: Enslow Publishers, 2013.

Richmond, Margie Hayes, ed. *Look What You Can Make with Paper Plates: Creative Crafts from Everyday Objects*. Honesdale, Penn.: Highlights Press, 2013.

Internet Sites

FactHound offers a safe, fun way to find Internet sites related to this book. All of the sites on FactHound have been researched by our staff.

Here's all you do:

Visit *www.facthound.com*

Type in this code: 9781476598970

Super-cool stuff! Check out projects, games and lots more at www.capstonekids.com